Growing
in
God

Daily Devotions to Fertilize Your Soul

Anita Colter

claypenpress

IOWA USA

Growing in God ~ Daily Devotions to Fertilize Your Soul

Table of Contents

Dedication

To my Lord and Savior, Jesus Christ,
for without Him I would have no hope.

*"If you can believe,
all things are possible to him who believes."*
Mark 9:23

Introduction

Do you want to live a victorious life? I believe you can! As you read these devotions, my prayer for you is that you are encouraged and that you grow in your relationship with Jesus Christ. Also, I pray you will fulfill the call that God has on your life and that you will get more victory in your life every day.

~ Anita Colter

Be Thankful

...in everything give thanks; for this is the will of God in Christ Jesus for you.
I Thessalonians 5:18

We should be giving thanks to God, for all things, all of the time. This is His will for us. When we wake up in the morning, the first thing we should do is start thanking the Lord and praising Him (Psalm 100:4). This is how we should start our prayer time.

Jesus is worthy of all our praise! Thank Him for what He has done, thank Him for what He is doing, and thank Him for what He is about to do. Thank Him as though He has already answered your prayers.

Do not grumble and complain (Philippians 2:14). The devil will try and tell you how bad everything is in your life and get you to complain. If you do this, it will only hold you back and keep God's blessings from flowing in your life (Numbers 14:26-30).

Keep a thankful, grateful, heart before the Lord. Keeping a gratitude journal will help you to focus on all the good God has done in your life.

Father, I ask that You help me to thank You in all things. When I am tempted to complain, help me to keep my mouth shut. Let the words of my mouth, and the meditation of my heart be acceptable in your sight (Psalm 19:14). In Jesus' name, amen.

Identity in Christ

If then you were raised with Christ, seek those things which are above, where Christ is, sitting at the right hand of God. Set your mind on things above, not on things on the earth. For you died, and your life is hidden with Christ in God.

Colossians 3:1-3

Do not try to get your value in things. You feel better about yourself because you live in a certain house, or you drive a particular car, or because of how much money you make. When you do that, you are trying to get your self-worth and value in things. You need to have stuff to make you feel better about yourself and who you are. Do not look to the world for fulfillment; Jesus is the only one that can do that for you.

You do not need things to make you feel better about yourself and to give yourself value. Everything you need is found in Christ. You are a child of the Most High God. He has crowned you with glory and honor (Psalm 8:5). You are forgiven, you are redeemed, you are worthy, and you are secure. You are a chosen generation, a royal priesthood, and a holy nation (1 Peter 2:9). You do not need stuff to make you feel better about yourself. You are better because of Jesus.

Father, help me when I am chasing after things to realize that is not what I need. What I need is more of You. Help me to come to You and get filled up with more of You, for You are the only One who can satisfy and fulfill me. Thank You for who I am in Christ. In Jesus' name, amen.

How to be Content

*Not that I speak in regard to need, for I have learned in whatever state
I am, to be content: I know how to be abased, and I know how to abound.
Everywhere and in all things I have learned both to be full and to be
hungry, both to abound and to suffer need.*

Philippians 4:11-12

You can learn how to be content. No matter what your situation is, you can be content! Whether you have a lot or whether you have a little. If you focus on what you do not have, instead of what you do have, it will cause you to be dissatisfied, frustrated, ungrateful, complaining, and negative. This can lead to anger and depression. That is where the devil wants to keep you!

God wants you to be thankful in all things; this is His will for you (1 Thessalonians 5:18). This pleases God when you are thankful. There is always something to be grateful for! When you are grateful, you will have more peace and joy in your life.

When you are waiting for God to move in a situation in your life, be content in the wait. Look at what you already have, and remember the things God has already done for you. Be patient, have faith, and trust Him in the wait. God will bring it to pass in His timing. In the meantime, continue to be faithful where God has placed you (Galatians 6:9).

*Father, please help me to be content no matter what is
going on in my life. Help me to trust that You are working
things out for my good in Your perfect timing.
In Jesus' name, amen.*

Priorities and Balance

And Jesus answered and said to her, "Martha, Martha, you are worried and troubled about many things. But one thing is needed, and Mary has chosen that good part, which will not be taken away from her."

Luke 10:41-42

It is easy to get busy serving God and saying yes to everything. Are you really supposed to be doing everything you are doing? If you are serving all of the time, but not taking time to read your Bible, pray, and be still before the Lord, you may need to pray about your priorities, and ask God to help you get a balance in your life. If you are too busy doing things for the Lord, but do not have time for Him because of it, you may need to make an adjustment in your schedule. The most important thing is your relationship with Jesus Christ and His will in your life (Matthew 7:21-23).

If you have a hard time saying no, you will find yourself over committed and overwhelmed. Learn to pray about everything, and be led by God (Jeremiah 33:3). This will help you keep your priorities straight and a balance in your life. This will also keep you from doing things that you are not supposed to be doing. There can be seasons where you will be busier than other seasons. Just make sure during the busier seasons, you are busy because God has you doing things. Make sure you are not doing things for the wrong reason. When you say yes, make sure you are saying yes for the right reason.

Father, life can be busy, someone or something always seems to need my attention. Help me to pray and ask You before I commit to anything. Show me what Your will is for me and help me to do it. If I am doing anything You do not want me to be doing, please show me. Help me to keep my priorities straight, with You being first, and a balance in every area of my life. In Jesus' name, amen.

God's Love Is not Rejection

For I am persuaded that neither death nor life, nor angels nor principalities nor powers, nor things present nor things to come, nor height nor depth, nor any other created thing, shall be able to separate us from the love of God which is in Christ Jesus our Lord.

Romans 8:38-39

Rejection will tell you everything you are not. God's love will tell you everything you are. Rejection causes you to feel unwanted, unaccepted, and unloved. Rejection will cause you to try and perform perfectly, try and please man, and try to get man's approval. You think you will be loved if you do everything perfectly. You think if you please man, and he approves of you, that you will be wanted and accepted. Nothing could be further from the truth. God already loves you (Jeremiah 31:3). You are loved, cherished, valued, and accepted in Christ Jesus.

God doesn't expect you to perform perfectly. His love for you is not based on your performance. God loves you for who you are, not what you do. The good news is He loves you unconditionally! You are accepted in the Beloved (Ephesians 1:6).

You do not have to fear rejection, you do not have to fear man, and you do not have to fear failure. You are enough, and you are accepted! God's love will never fail you. He is with you always. You will never be alone. He will never leave you (Deuteronomy 31:8).

Father, help me not to listen to the devil when he tells me I am not good enough. Thank You that I do not have to perform perfectly, or be approved by man to be loved and accepted. Thank You that I am enough, the real me, the me You created me to be. Thank You that You love and accept me just the way I am. In Jesus' name, amen.

Guard Your Heart

For out of the abundance of the heart the mouth speaks.
Matthew 12:34

Whatever is in your heart is going to come out of your mouth. That is why it is so important what you think on; whatever is in your mind, will eventually go to your heart. Whatever is in your heart, will eventually come out of your mouth.

You have to guard your heart from wrong thoughts, from things you are allowing yourself to hear, and from the words you are speaking. What you are thinking, hearing, and speaking will go to your heart; whatever is in your heart, you will speak out of your mouth. We need to be mindful of the things we are watching, reading, and listening to.

The things you meditate on are going to come out of your heart (Proverbs 4:23). Look at, listen to, and think on the things that are going to build you up and glorify God!

Father, help me to guard my heart today. Help me to watch the things I am letting in through my eyes and ears. Help me to be wise with the things I am looking at and listening to; let them glorify You. Help me to stay out of wrong conversations and not to get involved in gossiping. Instead, help me to focus on You and what Your Word says. In Jesus' name, amen.

Do not Fear!

Whenever I am afraid, I will trust in You. In God (I will praise His word), in God I have put my trust; I will not fear. What can flesh do to me?

Psalm 56:3-4

Fear is the opposite of faith. When we are in fear we are not trusting God. Fear is to flight (run away), but faith is to stay (stand), trust, and believe what God says.

The devil is always trying to get you to fear! Fear of failure, fear of man, fear of rejection, fear of what people think, fear of the future, and fear of lack. The devil will use fear to keep you from moving forward into what God has called you to do. If he can not stop you, he will try and slow you down. Do not listen to him! He is the father of lies (John 8:44).

God tells us to not be afraid and that He is with us wherever we go (Joshua 1:9). Keep your eyes on the Lord, trust in Him, step out in faith as He speaks to you, and you will be blessed!

Father, when fear comes in, help me not to be afraid. Help me to trust You and step out in faith as You speak to me. Thank You that You are with me always. In Jesus' name, amen.

God Gives Us Strength

He gives power to the weak, and to those who have no might He increases strength. Even the youths shall faint and be weary, and the young men shall utterly fall, but those who wait on the Lord shall renew their strength; they shall mount up with wings like eagles, they shall run and not be weary, they shall walk and not faint.

Isaiah 40:29-31

There are times when you do not feel like you will have enough strength to get you through the day. Today may be one of those days that you just need more strength. When you are trying to do it in your own strength, you will run out of steam. Take time to sit before the Lord, draw near to Him, and He will renew your strength.

Do not worry about the strength you will need for tomorrow. As each day comes, God will give you the strength to do what you need to do in that day. God is your strength (Habakkuk 3:19). It is Christ who gives you strength to do whatever it is He is asking you to do (Philippians 4:13).

Father, please give me the strength to do everything I need to do in this day. Thank You, Lord, that You are my strength, and I am strong in You. In Jesus' name, amen.

Peace not Confusion

For God is not the author of confusion but of peace,
as in all the churches of the saints.

1 Corinthians 14:33

When you are praying about a situation in your life, and you are waiting on direction from God, wait until you hear from God or have peace about the situation before you move on it. If you are feeling confused, that is not God. The devil will try and come in to cause confusion in your mind. When this happens, refocus your mind on Jesus and continue to pray until you have peace (John 14:27).

Do not run ahead of God; wait on Him. When you get inpatient, and do not wait on God, it will end up causing you problems. It can cause you to take the long way around. God is never early or late; He is always right on time. God's timing is perfect! Wait until He tells you to move and then you need to move. Do not stay back in fear! (Isaiah 41:10)

Father, I ask that You help me to wait on You and Your
perfect timing before I move. Help me to be lead by Your
peace. You know what is best for me. Help me to trust
You and Your timing. Not my will be done, but Your will
be done in me. In Jesus' name, amen.

Power in Unity

"Again I say to you that if two of you agree on earth concerning anything that they ask, it will be done for them by My Father in heaven. For where two or three are gathered together in My name, I am there in the midst of them."

Matthew 18:19-20

There is power in prayer and unity. There is power in being in agreement with others in prayer. It will benefit you to have a prayer partner, someone to stand in agreement with you in prayer. It is good to have people in your life that will be there to encourage you when you are going through stuff. It helps to know that you are not in it alone; God never intended for us to do life on our own. God is there for us, so we can be there for others (2 Corinthians 1:3-4).

Find someone you can trust, who you can share your heart with, that will keep in confidence what you say to them. Find someone that will stand in prayer, agreeing with you, and be there for you no matter what; then watch and see your prayers being answered! (Mark 11:24)

Father, thank You that You are always here for me. Help me to be there for others when they need encouragement. Thank You that You hear me when I pray. In Jesus' name, amen.

God's Love

For God so loved the world that He gave His only begotten Son, that whoever believes in Him should not perish but have everlasting life.

John 3:16

We were created to worship God, and be in relationship with Him. Sin separated us from God. He loved us so much that He sent His Son, Jesus, to die on the cross for our sins. Jesus bridged the gap for us so we could be forgiven and have a relationship with God.

The greatest gift God ever gave us was His Son, Jesus; without Him we would be destined to eternal damnation. We would have no hope. God, in all His grace, had mercy on us. He sent Jesus to die in our place and take all of our sins upon Himself. He died a cruel and horrible death for us. He conquered death, the grave, and hell for us. He rose from the dead on the third day. Jesus is seated at the right hand of God, and He sent His Holy Spirit to lead us and guide us in this lifetime. The only way to heaven is through Jesus (John 14:6).

If you have not received Jesus into your heart, He is waiting for you (2 Peter 3:9). Pray the prayer of salvation below today! (2 Corinthians 6:2)

God, I am a sinner. I need a Savior, and I believe that Savior is You, Jesus. God, I believe Jesus is Your Son. I believe He died on the cross for my sins, that He was buried, and You raised Him from the dead (Romans 10:9-10). I repent of my sins. Jesus, come into my heart and wash me clean. I turn from my sins and turn towards You. Thank You, Lord Jesus, for saving me.
In Jesus' name, amen.

Forgiveness

For if you forgive men their trespasses, your heavenly Father will also forgive you. But if you do not forgive men their trespasses, neither will your Father forgive your trespasses.

Matthew 6:14-15

We must forgive if we want God to forgive us. When you get angry, learn to let things go. Do not let your anger get the best of you. Anger, if not dealt with, can turn into bitterness, and then bitterness can turn into unforgiveness. We need to continually be forgiving of one another. Jesus said **we must forgive seventy times seven (Matthew 18:21-22).** When someone does something to offend you, let it go, do not hold onto anger.

When you have unforgiveness in your heart, it is not hurting the other person, it is only hurting you. When you forgive, it helps you, not the other person. You need to let it go; let go of the anger, let go of the bitterness, and forgive one another (Ephesians 4:31-32).

Not only do you need to forgive others, you need to forgive yourself. When you sin, repent, and God forgives you (Psalm 32:5). Receive God's forgiveness today.

Father, help me when I get angry to let it go. Help me to be a forgiving person and to forgive quickly. Thank You, Lord, that You are not only helping me to forgive others, but also helping me to forgive myself. In Jesus' name, amen.

Healing Is for You

...who Himself bore our sins in His own body on the tree, that we, having died to sins, might live for righteousness–by whose stripes you were healed.

1 Peter 2:24

Jesus paid a horrible price on the cross for our sins. He also took stripes on his back for our healing. God's will for you is to be healthy and whole, physically and emotionally. Sickness is a curse of the law. Jesus took all of our curses when He hung on the cross (Galatians 3:13).

Jesus is the great Physician! If you get a bad report from the doctor, you do not have to agree with it. Speak forth God's Word over your body; He heals all of your diseases (Psalm 103:3).

Jesus said, **"The thief does not come except to steal, and to kill, and to destroy. I have come that they may have life, and that they may have it more abundantly." (John 10:10)** If you need a healing, speak these scriptures over your body, stand in faith, and trust that God's will for you is to be healed.

Father, I thank You that by Jesus' stripes I am healed. Thank You, Jesus, that You heal me of all diseases. I thank You that I am healed from the top of my head, to the soles of my feet. In Jesus' name, amen.

Let God do the Work

...being confident of this very thing, that He who has begun a good work in you will complete it until the day of Jesus Christ...

Philippians 1:6

When we come to Christ we come with all of our baggage and issues. It is our job to submit to God and His job to clean us up. You may not always be able to see that you have an issue, so be open to whatever God is showing you about yourself. Allow Him to come in, and do the work that needs to be done in you. You will need to cooperate with the Holy Spirit, and do whatever it is He is asking you to do. This is a lifetime process of God sanctifying and purifying you; He takes you from glory to glory (2 Corinthians 3:18).

Many of us look good on the outside, but on the inside we are broken. We do not want others to see how fearful and insecure we are. Things have happened to you, in your life, to cause you to feel this way. You think the real you is not good enough and that people will not accept the real you. Allow God to come in and restore you. We are all broken people. Let God do the work that needs to be done in you (Psalm 34:19). He wants to use you to help someone else through this process, but first you have to let God do the work in you.

Father, help me to deal with the things You are showing me about myself. I invite You in to do the work that needs to be done in me. I thank You, Lord, that You are restoring me and making me whole. In Jesus' name, amen.

Dealing with Disappointment

Blessed is the man who trusts in the Lord,
and whose hope is in the Lord.

Jeremiah 17:7

There are times when life can have its disappointments: you did not get the job you hoped for; the loan did not come through on the house you wanted to buy; you did not get into the college you wanted to go to; the person you thought you were going to marry broke up with you. When you go through disappointments in life, trust that the Lord has something better for you, and put your hope in Him.

You have your mind and heart set on something; when it doesn't work out the way you planned, God's got something better for you (Proverbs 16:9). His ways are always better than your ways (Isaiah 55:9). When one door closes another will open. Do not be discouraged–God has something so much better for you! (Ephesians 3:20)

Father, I thank You that when things do not go the way I had planned, that You have something better for me. I trust that You are working all things out for me today. In Jesus' name, amen.

Where Are You God?

For the eyes of the Lord are on the righteous, and His ears are open to their prayers; but the face of the Lord is against those who do evil.

1 Peter 3:12

When you have been praying about something for a long time, and you have not heard from God, it is easy to think that He has forgotten about you. Is God listening to you when you pray? (Jeremiah 29:12). Does God hear you when you pray? Yes, He does hear you! (Psalm 18:6)

Have you ever cried out to God, "Where are you God?!" He is with us even when we do not feel Him; He is with us even when we are not hearing from Him. It is in the dry desert place that you have to keep pressing in. God may be growing your faith during this time. He may be teaching you to trust Him. God wants you to continue seeking Him and searching for Him with all of your heart (Jeremiah 29:13).

When God is silent, you do not have to wonder if He is with you. He cares about what is going on in your life. Be assured, God cares about every detail of your life (1 Peter 5:7).

Father, I thank You that You hear me when I pray. Help me to keep pressing in, even when I am not hearing from You. Help me to learn what You are teaching me during this time. Thank You that You care about every detail of my life. In Jesus' name, amen.

New Mercies

Through the Lord's mercies we are not consumed, because His compassions fail not. They are new every morning; great is Your faithfulness.

Lamentations 3:22-23

This is a new day. The Lord's mercies are new every morning! There is new joy, new peace, and new strength. Everything you need for this day is found in Jesus. He is faithful!

Do not look back to yesterday, for it is over; leave the past in the past. Whatever sins you may have done or whatever mistakes you may have made, repent and move on. Do not let the devil steal your joy today, over something that happened yesterday. Cast all your care onto the Lord (1 Peter 5:7). Do not look ahead to tomorrow; live each day as it comes. God has already gone into your tomorrow, and nothing that happens will surprise Him. God will be there to help you with whatever challenges you may face in that day. Live in this day the Lord has given you; enjoy this day to the fullest (Psalm 118:24).

Father, I ask that You help me not to worry about things that happened yesterday, and help me not to be anxious about tomorrow. As cares of this world try to come in today, help me to cast them onto You. I thank You that I will enjoy this day You have given me.
In Jesus' name, amen.

Love One Another

'You shall love your neighbor as yourself.'
Matthew 22:39

God tells us that we need to be loving people. We should be looking for people to bless. God wants to use us to show others how much He loves them. Allow God to use you to love someone today.

There are a lot of hurting people in this world that need to know God's love. We should be giving God's love away to others. There are so many ways to show God's love to others: you can love someone with a prayer, a smile, a hug, a card, a phone call, a visit, a word of encouragement, a compliment, a favor. These things may seem little and insignificant to you, but to the person on the receiving end it will mean so much more to them!

There are so many ways to love people. Let us not be so wrapped up in our own little world, that we do not notice those around us that need God's love. Be sensitive to the voice of the Holy Spirit speaking to you. When He asks you to love, it will usually cost you your time, talent, or money. We can be selfish at times, but we should be learning to put others before ourselves and be generous in our giving. You will get such a blessing out of being a blessing. You are always more blessed when you are giving (Acts 20:35). God gave us His love, so let us give His love away to others (1 John 4:11).

·•━·━■●■━·━•·

Father, I ask that You help me not to be too busy,
preoccupied, self-absorbed, or selfish to notice people
around me that need Your love. When You speak to me,
help me to hear You and obey.
In Jesus' name, amen.

Peaceful Mind

* * *

You will keep him in perfect peace, whose mind is stayed on You,
because he trusts in You.

Isaiah 26:3

There are many things in this life that can steal our peace: things are not going well at work, the children are misbehaving, a bad report from the doctor, having relationship difficulties, having financial problems. The good news is you do not have to let these things get you upset, get you down, or steal your peace. If you keep your mind and your focus on Jesus, He will keep you in perfect peace.

You have a choice to make: you can dwell on the problems or shift your focus onto God. As you pray and thank Him, your peace will return to you (Philippians 4:6-8). Jesus did not promise us a problem free life, but He did say we could have peace in the midst of our tribulations (John 16:33).

* * *

Father, I ask that You help me to keep my eyes on You today. When things that are going on in my life come in and try to steal my peace, help me to keep my mind stayed on You, so I will be in perfect peace. In Jesus' name, amen.

God Is Trustworthy

For the vision is yet for an appointed time; but at the end it will speak, and it will not lie. Though it tarries, wait for it; because it will surely come, it will not tarry.

Habakkuk 2:3

When God gives you a vision, there will be a waiting period. While you are waiting for Him to bring it to pass in your life, be patient during the wait. Do not run ahead of Him and try to make something happen before its time. Keep the faith, keep believing, and keep trusting in God; He will bring it to pass at the appointed time!

Never lose sight of who God is and what He can do for you. God will open doors of opportunity for you at the right time. He will bring the right people into your life at the right time; He will make a way where you do not see a way (Isaiah 43:19). Expect! Continue to expect God to do great things for you. He is faithful! (Psalm 119:90)

Father, help me to wait on You and Your timing. You have the big picture, and You know when I am ready for what You have for me. I thank You that I can trust You and Your timing. In Jesus' name, amen.

Giving to God

Bring all the tithes into the storehouse, that there may be food in My house, and try me now in this, says the Lord of hosts, if I will not open for you the windows of heaven and pour out for you such blessing that there will not be room enough to receive it.

Malachi 3:10

The tithe is the first ten percent of all your income. That is what belongs to God. We are actually robbing God if we are not tithing (Malachi 3:8). When you tithe, God not only promises to bless you, but also rebukes the devourer for you (Malachi 3:11). When you tithe, you are returning to God what is already His. When you do this, God will bless the ninety percent and will stretch it out for you. You will always have enough for all of your needs (Philippians 4:19).

When you give offerings, additional to your tithe, you are sowing a seed and you will reap what you sow (2 Corinthians 9:6-9). Give and it will be given to you (Luke 6:38). Whenever you give to God, whether it be your time, talent, or money, He will always bless you in return.

Father, help me not to worry or stress over money. As I give back to You, I thank You that I do not have to fear lack. You supply all of my needs. You are my Father, and You will take good care of me.
In Jesus' name, amen.

Cast ~ Rest ~ Trust

...casting all of your care upon Him, for He cares for you.
1 Peter 5:7

There are many situations in life that can cause you to have anxiety, fear, worry, or stress. While you are waiting on God to move on your behalf, in whatever the situation may be, God wants you to cast your cares on Him and leave them there.

Rest in Him; that means to not worry about it or try and figure it out (Psalm 46:10). If you are struggling, working, and trying to make it happen, you are not resting. Leave it in God's capable hands. He has got it! He does not need your help.

Trust that God knows what is best for you. He will not let you down (Proverbs 3:5-6). In His perfect time, He will work it out for you. God is never early or late; He is always right on time. Do not be in a hurry; God is not. His job is to take care of it, your job is to relax, praise, and thank Him. Your answer is on its way. You can trust your Heavenly Father. He has got your best interest at heart.

Father, I ask that You help me to cast my cares onto You today. Help me to rest in You and not to worry. I trust that You are working things out for me. I praise You and thank You that You have already gone into my tomorrows, and the answer is on its way.
In Jesus' name, amen.

51

Victory in the Battle

You will not need to fight in this battle. Position yourselves, stand still and see the salvation of the Lord, who is with you, O Judah and Jerusalem! Do not fear or be dismayed; tomorrow go out against them, for the Lord is with you.

2 Chronicles 20:17

When you are going through difficulties in your life, and everything is coming against you; such as the car breaks down, the money is lacking, you get sick; when you have done everything you know to do, Stand! Stand on His promises. Stand still and see the salvation of the Lord. The battle belongs to the Lord. Worship the Lord and praise Him (2 Chronicles 20:18-19).

You are serving God with your time, talent, and money. You are doing everything you know to do, but the enemy is starting to wear you down. He is attacking your mind, your emotions, your body, your finances, and your marriage. Break through is coming! Do not give up! God is with you. He is fighting for you against your enemies (Deuteronomy 20:4). You have the victory in the battle. God always causes you to triumph (2 Corinthians 2:14).

Father, I thank You that You've got this; nothing is too difficult for You. I praise You, and I worship You. I thank You that You are with me, and that I have the victory in the battle. In Jesus' name, amen.

Watch What You Say

*Death and life are in the power of the tongue,
and those who love it will eat its fruit.*

Proverbs 18:21

It is so important to watch what we say. Your words are very powerful. They will either make you or break you. Your words are leading you on the path to failure and defeat, or they are leading you on the path to success and victory. It is better to keep your mouth shut and say nothing, than to speak death over your life.

The Bible has a lot to say about the words we are speaking out of our mouth. We need to chose our words wisely. Think about what you are saying before you say it. The next time you have the urge to complain or speak negatively, zip your lip! (Proverbs 10:19, 21:23)

Whatever you want to see happening in your life, that is what you need to be speaking over your life. Speak life! (Romans 4:17)

Father, help me with the words I am speaking out of my mouth. Help me to speak words of life and not words of death. Help me to keep my mouth shut rather than complain. In Jesus' name, amen.

Growing in Faith

Now faith is the substance of things hoped for,
the evidence of things not seen.

Hebrews 11:1

Having faith is believing in something you cannot see (2 Corinthians 5:7). You must have faith in order to please God. You need to believe that God exists and go to Him continually in prayer. When you do this, you will be rewarded (Hebrews 11:6). Pray and thank God in advance for what He is going to do for you. Stand on God's promises concerning what you are believing Him to do for you.

How do you get faith? Romans 10:17 tells us that, "…faith comes by hearing, and hearing by the Word of God." This is why it is so important to be in church, read your Bible, and listen to the Word of God. This is how you grow in your faith in God. The more Word you have in you, the bigger your faith is.

You need to believe that God answers your prayers when you pray. While you are waiting for Him to answer your prayers, trust and thank Him.

Father, help me to continually have faith in You. I want to be pleasing to You, and I want all the rewards You have for me. Help me not to doubt or listen to the lies of the enemy, but to stand on Your promises for me. Thank You that You hear me when I pray. In Jesus' name, amen.

Run Your Race

Therefore we also, since we are surrounded by so great a cloud of witnesses, let us lay aside every weight, and the sin which so easily ensnares us, and let us run with endurance the race that is set before us, looking unto Jesus, the author and finisher of our faith, who for the joy that was set before Him endured the cross, despising the shame, and has sat down at the right hand of the throne of God.

Hebrews 12:1-2

We all have our own race to run. Run your race, the race God has put before you. When we run up against things that cause us to sin, we need to repent and run back to Jesus. We get off course sometimes; when this happens redirect yourself back to Jesus. We need to keep our eyes on Jesus and continue to take steps of faith.

Do not worry about what you think God should be doing in another person's life or about what you think another person should be doing with their life. That is between them and God. He has unique things for each of us to do. We are all at a different place in our walk with God, and we all move at our own pace. His timing for what He has called me and you to do may be different. God has not called you to run another person's race. We all have our own race to run. You will have to answer to God on what you did on this earth, not what someone else did. Run your race! Keep pressing toward the goal (Philippians 3:14).

Father, help me to run the race You have set before me. Help me to keep my eyes on You, and help me to stay the course. Help me to keep my focus on what You are doing in my life and keep pressing toward the goal. In Jesus' name, amen.

59

Success not Failure

For I know the thoughts that I think toward you, says the Lord, thoughts of peace and not of evil, to give you a future and a hope.

Jeremiah 29:11

God has a good future for you! Do not look at how far you still need to go; look at how far you have come. Do not focus on your weaknesses, fears, or failures. Instead, focus on who you are in Jesus and how much He loves you. His love for you is everlasting and will never fail. God is molding you into His image a little bit at a time (Philippians 1:6). God knows your fears; talk to Him about them. Break the power over them by bringing them into the light and exposing them.

God wants you to listen to Him, and take steps of faith. As you do this, He will lead you into success for your life (Isaiah 55:8-9). You have everything you need to be a success. Jesus is in you and He is with you. You are who He says you are, and you can do what He says you can do.

Pray and ask God what the next step is and then obey Him. Your steps of obedience will take you into God's plan for your life one step at a time. Trust that God has a good outcome for your life, that He wants to do more than you can ask or think (Ephesians 3:20).

Father, thank you for how far I have come in you. Help me not to fear, help me to obey, and help me to take steps of faith as you lead me. In Jesus' name, amen.

Obedience

Do you not know that to whom you present yourselves slaves to obey, you are that one's slaves whom you obey, whether of sin leading to death, or of obedience leading to righteousness?

Romans 6:16

When God asks you to do something, do not let selfishness or fear keep you from obeying Him. You can choose to be slaves to selfishness and fear, or obey God and His ways. His ways are always best (Isaiah 55:9). When God speaks to you about doing something, you can choose to obey and be blessed, or disobey and forfeit your blessing (1 Samuel 15:22-23).

Sometimes you may not always understand why God is asking you to do something. He may be testing you to see if He can trust you with more. He may be trying to get a blessing to you (Matthew 25:20-21). God is trying to get you to where He wants you to go, but you have to trust Him and obey Him to get there.

Father, I thank You that You will help me to do things Your way and not my way. I thank You that You are helping me to trust and obey You more and more every day. In Jesus' name, amen.

Be Confident

...the Spirit of truth, whom the world cannot receive, because it neither sees Him nor knows Him; but you know Him, for He dwells with you and will be in you.

John 14:17

Learn to be confident in Jesus who lives in you. Jesus is in you and speaking to you all of the time. Listen to the promptings of the Holy Spirit. Step out when you hear Him speaking to you. Faith by itself is dead; you need to have works to back it up (James 2:20). Learn to trust Him in you. We walk not by how we feel, or what makes sense to us, or what we see, we walk by faith (2 Corinthians 5:7). As you do this, you will begin to have more confidence of Jesus in you.

Father, help me learn to trust You in me more and more. When You are speaking to me, help me to listen and step out in faith. In Jesus' name, amen.

You are Called

For we are His workmanship, created in Christ Jesus for good works, which God prepared beforehand that we should walk in them.

Ephesians 2:10

God created us for a purpose. We all have an assignment we need to complete here on this earth. When God calls you He has equipped you. You have everything in you to do what God has called you to do. God has called you to do great things. You have greatness in you just waiting to come out!

Get out of your head, and get out of the way. Nobody but you is stopping you from doing what God called you to do! Trust God in you, and be confident of Jesus in you. Do not listen to fear or the lies of the devil. Do not let the devil talk you out of what God has called you to do!

God wants to give you the desires of your heart (Psalm 37:4). He is the one that put them there. When you step out in faith and do your part, then God will do His part. You will have to be determined, disciplined, and focused to accomplish what God has called you to do. Determine in your heart that you will not quit! God has great rewards for you.

You will not be satisfied or fulfilled until you are walking in the plan that God has for your life. You can take a detour and slow it down, or you can cooperate with God and have it come to pass sooner in your life.

Father, help me get to where You want me to go. Help me to trust You more and not to fear. Help me to stay focused and fulfill the call that You have on my life. In Jesus' name, amen.

Pray and Listen

Then you will call upon Me and go and pray to Me, and I will listen to you.
Jeremiah 29:12

When you pray God listens to you. God not only wants you to pray to Him, but He also wants you to listen to what He is saying to you. Prayer is a two-way conversation. Pray and then listen to what God is saying to you. Learn to be still before Him so He can show you things (Jeremiah 33:3).

It can be hard, at times, to be still and listen to what God is saying to you. There may be distractions and your mind may start to think about something else that you need to do. When your mind starts to wander, redirect your focus back on the Lord.

You will need to find a quiet place to pray. Put a "Do Not Disturb" sign on the door. Turn off your cell phone and all your social media. Do whatever you have to do so you can have your quiet time with the Lord!

It is so important to listen to what God is saying to you. When you start to hear His still, small voice, He will lead you into His will for your life. Journal what God is speaking to you so that you can go back and see what He spoke to you over time.

Father, I ask that You help me take the time to pray to You every day. Help me to be still and listen to what You are saying to me. Help me to guard this time with You so I can grow in my relationship with You and become the person You have called me to be. In Jesus' name, amen.

Waiting on God

I wait for the Lord, my soul waits, and in His word I do hope.
Psalm 130:5

God speaks to you about what He is calling you to do. Now, you are waiting for Him to open the doors of opportunity for you. You do not understand why it has not happened yet. It can be hard waiting on God; when you do not see anything happening, you are tempted to give up and quit. When doubt and discouragement come in, encourage yourself in His Word; put your hope in Him (Psalm 13:1-6). Trust Him in the wait–do not give up!

While you are waiting, God is doing a work in you. He is preparing you for promotion and getting you ready for the next level. He is growing your faith in Him; God is getting you stronger so that you will be able to handle everything that goes along with what He has called you to do. God is testing you during this time to see if He can trust you with more. Continue to wait on the Lord, and He will strengthen your heart (Psalm 27:14).

Father, I know that You have good things in store for me. Help me not to give up and continue to trust You in the wait. In Jesus' name, amen.

Manage Your Time

See then that you walk circumspectly, not as fools but as wise, redeeming the time, because the days are evil. Therefore do not be unwise, but understand what the will of the Lord is.

Ephesians 5:15-17

God wants us to manage our time well. Find out what the will of the Lord is for your life, and then go after it with all that is in you. You need to be aware of distractions and procrastination! Satan will try to use them to keep you out of God's will for your life. He wants to slow you down or stop you from doing what God has called you to do.

Be mindful of things that steal your time and suck you in, such as when you are on your phone all the time, on social media, or bingeing on Netflix. These things are okay when done in moderation, but as with everything, balance is the key. You know that you are out of balance in an area, when you are spending most of your time on one particular thing. God wants us to use good time management. You will need that in order to do the things He has called you to do. We all have the same amount of time in a day; what you accomplish with it is up to you. Life is so short; be wise with your time (Psalm 90:12).

Father, help me to use my time wisely and manage my time well. When I am out of balance, bring me back into balance. Help me use self-control and discipline in every area of my life. In Jesus' name, amen.

God Is . . .

*Blessed be the Lord, Who daily loads
us with benefits, The God of our salvation!*
Psalm 68:19

God is the Great I Am. (Exodus 3:14)

He is the God Most High. (Psalm 97:9)

He is the God of abundance. (Ephesians 3:20)

He is the God of more than enough. (2 Corinthians 9:8)

He is the God of restoration. (Joel 2:25)

He is the God of peace. (John 14:27)

He is the God of joy. (Psalm 16:11)

He is the God of love. (1 John 4:9)

He is the God of mercy. (Luke 6:36)

He is the God of grace. (Ephesians 1:7)

He is the God of strength. (Psalm 46:1)

He is the God of healing. (Isaiah 53:5)

He is the God of prosperity. (3 John 1:2)

He is the God in whom all blessings flow. (James 1:17)

In God there is everything you need. Go to Him and He will fill you up. Go to God and He will give you all you need!

*Father, I thank You for all the blessings I have in You!
Thank You for saving me and loving me.
In Jesus' name, amen.*

Keep Believing

When you pass through the waters, I will be with you; and through the rivers, they shall not overflow you. When you walk through the fire, you shall not be burned.

Isaiah 43:2

When you are walking through the fire, know that God is with you. He will keep your head above the water no matter what you are going through. You are blessed, you are cherished, and you are not alone. God is with you always (Matthew 28:20).

When we are going through difficult situations in our lives, and we are not hearing from God, we can start to think that God has forgotten about us. During these times we need to press in and keep believing, keep trusting, and keep walking by faith. God is working even when we do not see it (2 Corinthians 5:7). Say, "I trust you Jesus." Do not stop believing. God is making a way. He has not forgotten you!

Father, help me when I feel like I am not going to make it, to lift my eyes to You. Thank You, God, that I am not alone, and You have not forgotten about me. I will keep believing, keep trusting, and keep walking by faith. In Jesus' name, amen.

Let Go of Control

Oh Lord of hosts, blessed is the man who trusts in you!
Psalm 84:12

When you trust in God, you will be blessed! This is not always easy to do, especially if you have control issues. When you have control issues, your tendency is not to trust. You do not trust God to take care of you. You are afraid He will not come through for you. You feel that you need to take care of yourself. God will take care of you (Philippians 4:19).

When you try and control things and make them go your way, you are not trusting God. If you are struggling, working, and trying to make things happen in your own strength, you are not trusting God (Zechariah 4:6). You need to sit back, relax, and rest in God. You will have more peace as you trust in Him and His perfect timing.

If you are feeling pushed and driven, that is not God. He is a leader and a guider, not a pusher and driver. God wants you to let go of control and trust in Him (Psalm 34:8). You can not control everything in your life no matter how hard you try. Things happen in life that are beyond your control. Trust your Heavenly Father to take care of you. He has only good things in store for you!

Father, help me to let go of control, and help me not to do things in my own strength. Help me to relax and trust You to take care of me. I thank You that You have good things in store for me. In Jesus' name, amen.

Prosperity

"Let the Lord be magnified, who has pleasure in the prosperity of His servant."

Psalm 35:27

God's will for us is to prosper. He takes pleasure when we prosper. God wants us to prosper in everything that we do. He wants us to prosper in our careers, our businesses, our ministries, our marriages, our families, and in our relationships. He wants us to prosper in all things in our lives (3 John 1:2).

As God prospers us, and we give back to His kingdom, He will continue to give us more so that we can give more (Proverbs 11:24 -25). We can help more and more people. We can bring the love of Jesus and His hope to lost and hurting people. That is what it is all about! God blesses us so we can be a blessing (Proverbs 22:9).

Draw near to God, listen to Him, and obey whatever it is He is asking you to do. He will never steer you wrong. God wants to bless you, but He also wants to use you to bless others. Be a generous giver!

Father, thank You that You want to prosper me in everything that I do. As You prosper me, I thank You that I can give back to Your kingdom and more people will know Your love because of it. In Jesus' name, amen.

Jesus Defines You

Therefore, if anyone is in Christ, he is a new creation; old things have passed away; behold, all things have become new.

2 Corinthians 5:17

You are a new creation in Christ Jesus. Do not let who you are be defined by . . .

- your past
- what happened to you
- your own perception of yourself
- other people's perception of you
- the world
- the devil's lies

God is the only one who gets to define who you are. The only truth of who you are is who God says you are. You are not what you did. You are not what happened to you. You are a child of the Most High God! (Psalm 82:6)

God created you for a special purpose. He had something specific in mind for you when He created you (Ephesians 2:10). God has started a good work in you and He will finish it! (Philippians 1:6)

Father, thank You that I am a child of the Most High God, and You created me for a purpose. Thank You that You will complete the work You started in me. In Jesus' name, amen.

Rejoice ~ Pray ~ Thank

This is the day the Lord has made; we will rejoice and be glad in it.

Psalm 118:24

Rejoice and be glad in this day God has given you! When you wake up in the morning, and you do not feel ready to conquer the day, this may not be the first thing you feel like doing; your mind starts to race as you think about all the things you need to do in this day. You may not have slept well, or you may not feel well. The devil starts telling you lies about how bad everything is in your life. You are already starting to feel defeated, and the day has barely begun. This is when you need to rejoice the most. Start rejoicing, praising, and worshiping God; His joy, peace, and strength will return to you. You will be able to pray and give thanks to God and will have a better perspective on the day ahead. You have the victory over this day! (1 Corinthians 15:57)

Father, I thank You for this day You have given me. I choose to rejoice and be glad in it! I praise You for who You are and for everything You have done for me. Thank You that I will enjoy this day.
In Jesus' name, amen.

Help Me Jesus!

I will lift up my eyes to the hills—from whence comes my help? My help comes from the Lord, who made heaven and earth.

Psalm 121:1-2

When you need help, Jesus is always there for you. He is near to you; He is just a prayer away. When you are having a hard time or a rough day, just say, "Jesus help me!"

There will be days that you need His help. Do not hesitate to ask Him for help. Jesus wants you to invite Him into every part of your life. He cares about every detail in your life, no matter how big or small it is. He is a merciful God. He wants to help you, but you have to ask Him for help (Hebrews 4:15-16).

God longs to help you; He is your Heavenly Father. What good father doesn't want to help his child? Cry out to God; He is there for you. He wants to help you. God did not intend for you to do this life on your own. As long as you try to do it on your own, He will watch you struggle. He is waiting for you to come to Him and ask for help (James 4:7-8, 10).

Father, help me to come boldly before Your throne of grace, that I may obtain mercy and find grace to help in time of need (Hebrews 4:16). In Jesus' name, amen.

Do not Worry

Therefore do not worry about tomorrow, for tomorrow will worry about its own things. Sufficient for the day is its own trouble.

Matthew 6:34

Jesus tells us not to worry. Every day can bring new problems. Live in the day you are in. Rely on God to get you through each day as it comes.

Do not borrow problems, worry about things that will probably never happen, or things that are beyond your control; all this does is steal your peace and joy. Jesus said, **"Peace I leave with you, My peace I give to you; not as the world gives do I give to you. Let not your heart be troubled, neither let it be afraid." (John 14:27)** Do not let the devil steal your joy. Say, "No! Not today, devil!"

When tomorrow arrives your Heavenly Father will be there to see you through whatever that day brings. Trust Him to take care of you. Live in the here and now, and enjoy this day God has given you!

Father, I ask that You help me not to worry about anything today. I cast my cares onto You. I thank You that You are in control of every situation and every circumstance in my life. I trust that You are working all things out for my good today.
In Jesus' name, amen.

Devil Is Defeated!

Finally, my brethren, be strong in the Lord and in the power of His might.
Ephesians 6:10

Do not look at everything that is going bad in your life as a defeat. When you are going through trials and tribulations and the devil is attacking you, look at these things as stepping stones to where you are going–to where God is taking you. God is using these things to grow you, stretch you, and make you stronger (1 Corinthians 16:13).

When you are having a bad day; you are struggling in the midst of a battle and you do not feel like you are going to make it, remember that the devil is under your feet. You have power over him; nothing will harm you (Luke 10:19).

You have the victory in Jesus' name! The devil is defeated (1 John 4:4). It doesn't matter how you feel. Fix your eyes on Jesus; lift up your praise and worship to Him.

Father, I ask that You help me when the devil tries to discourage me, tell me lies, and get me to quit. Give me the strength to fight back and speak what Your Word says about me. Help me to sing praises and worship You in the midst of the battle. I thank You that I have the victory. In Jesus' name, amen.

Control Your Thoughts

...casting down arguments and every high thing that exalts itself against the knowledge of God, bringing every thought into captivity to the obedience of Christ...

2 Corinthians 10:5

You have control over your mind. You do not have to agree with every thought that comes into your mind; when wrong thoughts come in, you do not have to think on them. If these thoughts do not line up with what the Word of God says about you, cast them down and out. Then you need to replace those thoughts with what God's Word says about you.

This will take practice. You have to be aware of what you are thinking about. When you realize you are thinking on the wrong thoughts, immediately replace those thoughts with God's Word (Romans 12:2). You have to reprogram your mind and learn a new way of thinking. It is like when you hear something on the radio you do not want to hear, you can change the station to something you do want to hear! We are to meditate on good things (Philippians 4:8).

Father, when wrong, negative, accusing thoughts come into my mind, I ask that You help me to cast them down and out quickly. Help me to replace them with what You say about me and think on whatever is true, noble, just, pure, lovely, and a good report. In Jesus' name, amen.

Protection

No weapon formed against you shall prosper, and every tongue which rises against you in judgment You shall condemn. This is the heritage of the servants of the Lord, and their righteousness is from Me, says the Lord.

Isaiah 54:17

A weapon may form against you, but it will not prosper because you are a servant of the Lord and you are made right with God through Jesus. You are protected. God will take care of you and protect you. He is your protector! You do not have to fear sickness, disease, or harm. He gives His angels charge over you to keep you in all your ways (Psalm 91:11).

When you wake up in the morning, plead the blood of Jesus over yourself, your family, your vehicle, and over any place you will be that day. Be at peace, and trust that God is protecting you. We live in this world, but we are not of this world. We are children of the Most High God. We are covered under Him. Read Psalm 91 today. It is all about safety of abiding in the presence of God.

Father, I thank You for Your hand of protection over me today. Thank You that no sickness, disease, or harm will come near me or my family. In Jesus' name, amen.

Keeping Your Joy

Do not sorrow, for the joy of the Lord is your strength.

Nehemiah 8:10

It is so important to keep your joy; when you lose your joy, you lose your strength. Things can begin to feel hard and pressed down. You can start to feel a heaviness, and depression will try to creep in. This is the enemy's way of trying to keep you down, but you have the victory! (2 Corinthians 4:8-9)

So how do you keep your joy? Psalm 16:11 tells us that ...in God's presence is fullness of joy... so if you stay in God's presence, you will have His joy. I believe the way you do that is by fixing your mind and heart on Him. Throughout the day thank, praise, and worship God (Hebrews 13:15).

Some days it will be a battle and a struggle. You may not feel the Lord's joy right away, but as you continue to praise and worship the Lord, you will feel His joy rise up in you again! You will have strength to do what you need to do in this day.

Father, I ask that You help me today to keep the joy of the Lord. When the devil comes and tries to steal my joy, help me to praise and worship You. I thank You for giving me victory in the battle. In Jesus' name, amen.

About the Author

ANITA COLTER has walked with God for many years, but she struggled with knowing what His plan was for her life. As she began to seek God on a deeper level, He started to stir things in her heart. She continued to pray about discovering the purpose He had created her for. God started to reveal His plan for her life, and part of that plan was to write this devotional. He has given her a heart towards ministry to women. She lives with her husband in Missouri.

claypenpress

fragile lives, strong stories.

claypenpress.com